Notes from the Editor

I am pleased to present to you Issue 3 of **Entrepreneur Platform Magazine.** For those of you that are reading for the first time, **WELCOME!** Our magazine is designed to bring out that gift, that entrepreneur that lives inside each of us.

Featured on the front cover is **Ms. Jasmine Roland**, Founder & CEO of Jazz Em Up Photography. Come get up close and personal with this extraordinary entrepreneur who overcame obstacles and setbacks to build her company from the ground and achieve success.

In this issue, you will also meet Award Winning Author, Business Keynote Speaker and Business Growth Expert, **Meridith Elliott Powell**. Meridith will teach you what it takes to thrive and remain profitable no matter what's going on with the economy. If you're new to the entrepreneur game or even a seasoned veteran, this article is for you.

Katie O'Reilly is back in the kitchen at Katie O's Food Carnival. It's is all about cooking healthy with the color "orange". Katie will take you into her kitchen via video tutorial and teach you step by step how to bring the healthy out of all foods orange. Her cookbook is also available in this issue.

Rhoda Johnson, Founder & CEO of Rhoda Design Group is back with her expertise, wisdom and tips for entrepreneurs on "Personal Branding Presence". If you think that how you present yourself and show up for business as an entrepreneur doesn't matter, then you won't be in business long. Enjoy!

Kelli M. Williams
Publisher

Disclaimer: The written and video content, views, opinions, suggestions and advise expressed in this magazine are solely those of the individuals providing them and do not reflect the opinions or advise of Entrepreneur Platform Magazine, LLC, its parent, affiliate or subsidiary companies.

Table of Contents

4 | *Thriving In Uncertainty*
5 Strategies To Succeed No Matter What This Economy Does
Meridith Elliott Powell

6 | Do You Take Risks To Reach New Heights?
Elinor Stutz

8 | 5 Reasons Why Your Facebook Posts Aren't Seen By More People And What To Do About It...
Karen Liz Albert

10 | My Little Secrets for Your Success
Gordon Tredgold

12 | Start Saving and Investing for Your Future Goals and Retirement Early
Paranda Davis

14 | Cooking Healthy With Everything Orange
Katie O'Reilly

15 | The Millionaire Maker Game

16 | Jasmine Roland "Say Cheese" Wilmington's Favorite Family Photographer
Angel A. Wellington

22 | Personal Branding Presence
Rhoda Johnson

23 | Discovering the Author Within"
Ophelia Uke

24 | Dotcom Secrets Book Review
Nikki Murrill

28 | The Unstoppable Millionaire

29 | Well World Official

30 | Consultants

32 | Entrepreneurial Books of the Month

33 | Ripple and XRP

Contributors

MERIDITH ELLIOTT POWELL

PARANDA DAVIS

OPHELIA UKE

ELINOR STUTZ

ANGEL A. WELLINGTON

NIKKI MURRILL

KAREN LIZ ALBERT

KATIE O'REILLY

TAHIR HUSSAIN

GORDON TREDGOLD

RHODA JOHNSON

STERLING WELLINGTON

Thriving In Uncertainty
5 Strategies To Succeed No Matter What This Economy Does
Meridith Elliott Powell

Welcome to the age of Uncertainty. Where the biggest challenge you face isn't the economy or change, it's trying to grow in a marketplace where you never know when the economy will shift, what changes that will bring, or when any of that will happen. Everyone seems so concerned with watching the news, listening to the experts, studying the economists and trying to determine if the economy is going up, or if it is going down. When the truth is, I think somewhere deep inside we all realize that it is not about whether the economy is up or down, it is more about understanding that it's different. Radically changed, and that things are never, I mean never going back to the way that they were.

In fact, economists agree, they say we have literally gong through an economic shift. Moving out of what is known as a push economy and into what is known as a pull economy. Now, take a breath, because I am not about to give you an Econ 101 Lesson. Because all you need to know, all you need to understand is that when you move out of a push and into a pull the consumer, your customer, they just moved into the position of control. They are calling the shots, they have all the power.

Think about the world we live into today. Globalization, advancements in technology, increasing competition. We could all sit in our houses, the comfort of our own homes, Google until our hearts are content, and have everything we want, everything we need, everything our little heart desires delivered right to our door. Guessing you do that right now, guessing that as you read this article, you're realizing you're the king or queen of amazon prime. The way we make decisions today, the way we gather information, the way we buy it has all changed. And while it may be funny to think about sitting at home in our underwear ordering things online, that fact remains that makes this an economy like none of us have ever lived in, worked in, let alone try to sell education products in before.

That makes this a marketplace, where no matter how unique, spectacular or amazing we believe our products or services are, they are just our ticket to entry. Without a strong product you don't even get to compete in today's marketplace. But products are only half of what is drawing the business to you, and even less of what keeps customers coming back.

If you want to thrive in today's marketplace, thrive in uncertainty, you have to understand is less about what you do and more about how you do it.

5 Strategies To Thrive In Uncertainty

1. Embrace Reality – Wouldn't it be great if someone would ride in on a white horse or click their heels three times and stabilize our economy? Let me be the first to say, "That ain't gonna happen!"

Our society, our culture, is literally going through a transition that is bringing about extreme change at all levels in the marketplace, and with it a whole new way of doing business. If you want to succeed, embrace your new reality. What made you successful in 2018 is not going to be enough to make you successful in 2019.

2. Focus on Values – Welcome to the age of integrity, and the economy where what you do is as important, if not more important, than what you say. As a professional you need to know who you are and what you stand for in order to attract, retain, and truly deepen client relationships.

Today's consumers want and expect more. With so much competition, and so many choices, your customers are looking for more than a great product; they are looking for a professional they can trust – people and companies they can build relationships with. If you want to thrive in uncertainty you need to define your values and integrate them into every level of your business development strategy.

3. Build Your Image – In today's marketplace you need to realize the sales cycle starts without you. When you set down to read this article, while you were finishing the first paragraph, your best customers, you prospect already started the buying cycle. Right now, they are online goggling for ideas, they are heading to a meeting to talk with other educators, or they are reading industry magazines were guru and experts are making recommendations. If your name is not coming up, if your company is not the one, they are talking about, then

> *You know change is coming – if you see it is creating opportunity, keep your head in the sand and it becomes your biggest threat.*

by the time you make the sales call you are already behind.

Thriving in uncertainty is about understanding you have to build your reputation and create buzz in the marketplace, so you can attract the business before you ask for the business.

4. Invest In Relationships – The only reason prospects choose you over the competition, the only reason customers come back is because they know you, they like you and they trust you. Your ability to thrive in uncertainty is directly tied to

Continued on page 27

Do You Take Risks to Reach New Heights?

Elinor Stutz

Are you wondering if it's time to work on reaching new heights? As we perform the same tasks in the same way, every day, year after year, we accomplish little. Even worse is when one becomes discontent with work and life in general. But when we take a strategic chance on something new, our story can change for the better.

Story-telling is the art form of movies and television. The title of one television show comes to mind, "Life in Pieces." When people ask about my work, I suggest the business effort comes in three distinct parts with a fourth potentially on the horizon.

Two highly talented entrepreneurs will confirm that success involves taking an occasional strategic risk. One built a multi-million dollar financial business and then sold her share. She is proud of the fact she grew the business her way and then sold her percentage to her partner. The other person grew tired of the corporate environment. Today, she is slowly but steadily building her event planning business.

In both examples, the women began without much knowledge of the business they envisioned. But with perseverance, ignoring the naysayers, and doing everything possible to become successful, they were both able to achieve success.

A sad tale of another person during one of the conversations left me heartbroken. The story became the groundwork of why my connection chose to leave corporate behind. The motivating factor for always striving to do better is about a woman who, upon retirement, said approximately the following: *"Thank goodness retirement is finally possible! I hated going to my job every day for thirty years."*

Imagine, thirty years enduring a job you despise. It is more than most can bear. The missing pieces were the motivation and determination to find a better way to make a living. Not ignoring the need for income, there is usually a way to overlap quitting a job while hunting for and accepting the new. The more difficult piece is motivating oneself enough to continue learning the new.

Highlights of the two conversations are:

- Motivation to always do better
- Seeing the wisdom in taking an occasional risk
- Working our way in our authentic style
- Connecting only with people of similar values and priorities
- Including community service work to help makea difference

What the three of us came to realize is that by remaining in sync with who we are, and seeking out alliances who hold similar values, are the critical enablers for us to reach new heights.

Soul Searching Is a Requirement Before Attempting to Reach New Heights

As an employee, think about all the people with whom you connect. And then consider the atmosphere around you:

- Do you feel there is a team effort or is everyone in the group to win by themselves
- Is management supportive and helpful or more dictatorial
- Are you fed up with work or do you look forward to it each day?

On occasion, we do find a job that encourages personal development, and we see the existing element of fun. Should this be the case, dedicate yourself to learning and advancing your craft.

Goal setting is essential for getting to the next level. Although you may be happy today, sometime in the future the way of doing things will change. *"Thinking about and planning for your future saves the day."*

Figure out if there is room for advancement or if a new job search is in order. Where you are today may not be the best time to change jobs, but the research you do will reveal what you need to learn next. In the meantime, keep moving forward by continually setting more challenging goals.

Entrepreneurship is another possibility. On several levels, it is far more satisfying, but it can also be far more stressful. The question of how you will earn money and recognizing everything you do not already know can be frightening. However, you never know what is possible if you do not try.

Before any significant change these steps help:

- Speak to those who have gone before you
- Research possibilities
- Create a brain trust of peers
- Consider a partnership
- Include an element of community service

All the while branding, establishing your personal brand, and marketing are essential for independent work. Now circle back to the need of aligning with people who hold

> *Seek out people with similar interests and a collaborative style*

similar values and priorities. Likewise, community service is a win for you and the community you choose to serve. A job done well by helping others will produce a loyal following and forthcoming testimonials.

Similar to successful selling, entrepreneurial or employment type work should never be one-sided. When we look at the bigger picture of everyone being accepted and heard, the outcome stands to be far more robust and move you to reach new heights.

Continued on page 26

5 Reasons Why Your Facebook Posts Aren't Seen By More People And What To Do About It...

KAREN LIZ ALBERT

Have you ever noticed that your Facebook business page updates are not appearing in the timeline of your Facebook followers? Wondering how Facebook determines whether or not they should show your updates in the timeline of your followers and how to influence those determining factors?

As a small business owner on a budget you want to get as much organic reach on each post as possible. Facebook's algorithm is a complex one, and one of their well-guarded secrets. However, over time, some key factors were identified that helps contribute to your organic reach:

1. A Facebook user's previous interactions with your page – have they liked, shared and/or commented previously on any of your posts? Then they're more likely to have your new posts appear in their feeds organically. So a great way to ensure those users continue to engage with your posts is to always like and respond to a user's post comment and consider mentioning and/or tagging those engaged users in a post that thanks them for their support. This will call their attention to your page and prompt a response to that post and most likely future posts as well.

2. A Facebook user's previous interactions with certain post types (i.e. videos, or images, or Facebook live). For example, the user that has engaged with your video posts, will see your video posts more in their newsfeed. So, review your Facebook business page analytics to see which types of posts are receiving the most response from your community and increase those types of posts as a part of your content strategy.

3. The interactions of Facebook people who saw your posts. Facebook starts by showing your new posts to a small set of your Facebook followers (based on the previous two points), if those people engage with your recent post (i.e. like, share, comment) then Facebook will start to show that post to more Facebook users. Also, based on a user's post activity is how much Facebook will show your post to other users. For example, on a scale of 1 to 10, a "like" on a post is equivalent to a 3 or 4, a "comment" on a post is equivalent to a 6 or 7, and a "share" is a 10. That is why it is recommended to instruct your followers to like, comment and share in your post captions.

4. Any complaints or negative feedback. If a Facebook user reports your post to Facebook or says they're not interested in content like this, then Facebook won't show that content to them anymore. So be sure your content is relevant and adds value to your Facebook followers. Consider using your Facebook Pages Feed to find relevant content, from other Facebook business pages in your industry or niche, that you can share to your page.

5. When was it posted? New content is the most interesting, the longer something is online, the higher probability that it is not that relevant anymore to your users. Another reason why it is important to ask your followers to like, comment and share to keep older posts alive and shown to more and more Facebook users. If you are doing a Facebook live, request those watching the recording of your Facebook live to type "Repeat" as a comment. This will help increase the longevity of your Facebook live post. Incorporate these five strategies into your daily Facebook marketing strategy. I think you'll be pleased with how quickly you will increase the engagement with your posts.

About the author:

Karen Liz Albert is the founder of Behind Your Curtain and has 20+ years marketing experience providing impactful social media marketing consulting, training and services to hundreds of business owners, real estate professionals and authors. She is the host of her WomenOnTV.tv show, "Behind Your Curtain" and is a regular guest on some of the top radio & podcast shows for entrepreneurs.

Download her free guide *"10 Ways To Boost Your Business Using Social Media"*: **http://byc.scion-social.com/eguide**

GORDON TREDGOLD

MY LITTLE SECRETS FOR YOUR SUCCESS

Start Small

The second step is to start realizing your goal. Surprisingly, for the majority of people, getting started is the hardest part. Why? Maybe they feel overwhelmed because they doubt themselves. But where do these doubts come from? We all hear two voices that can make us doubt ourselves and prevent us from getting on the right path.

The first is that inner voice, that little devil we all have on our shoulders, the one who tells us we're not good enough, that we do not have the talent or the time.

The second voice is external. It is the one of all the people around us who also tell us that it is not possible, that it will never happen, because we do not have the means.

But more often than not, they speaking about themselves, not us. They express their own doubts, their own fears, and we must not let our potential become a prisoner of their doubts . The best approach to overcome doubts is to start small.

Find something you can do and start there. When I decided to run my first marathon at the age 52, my two best friends told me I was too old, too fat to do it. Maybe they were right. 42km is a lot. But I found a program that started with 15 minutes of jogging a day during the first week. So the next day we ran 15 minutes, it was not much, it was not easy for us, but it was a beginning. You do not have to eat the elephant all at once, just start with a little bite

Find something to do, which is possible, to silence those negative voices. And if you are in a leadership position, be the angel on the other shoulder telling people that they can do it and they will succeed.

Often my client feels overwhelmed, they want to accomplish big goals, but they do not know where to start. So what to do? A friend gave me the advice on how to clean up after a big party. No matter the size of the mess - always start with the cutlery.

"But why the cutlery? Do they have something special?" I asked. "If you always start with cutlery, it gives you a clear starting point." she answered.

You do not have to think, it becomes a reflex, and you just start automatically.

We must go from thinking to action. Then, once you get started, things keep going.

So, for your big goal, ask yourself what little thing you can do and start there.

Only when we start, can we follow the paths to success.

PARANDA DAVIS

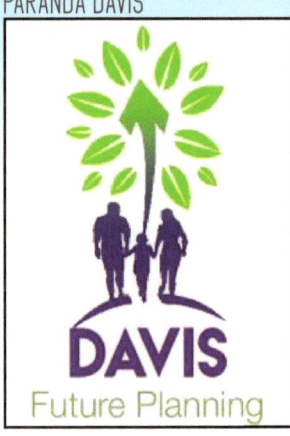

Start Saving and Investing for Your Future Goals and Retirement Early

Start Early

It's very important that you start saving or investing towards your future goals, including your retirement as soon as possible. Firstly, you need to decide what your goals are and then determine how soon you want to accomplish those goals.

Ask yourself, what are my short, medium and long-term objectives? Then start working on a plan towards achieving those goals.

Speak with a Financial Advisor/Planner

Seeking out investment opportunities can be intimidating, especially for first-time inexperienced investors. However, there are qualified financial advisors who can help put you on the right path towards achieving your financial objectives. Have a discussion with your Advisor regarding your goals and start building a road-map to achieve them.

How much you save or invest today can have a great impact on your future lifestyle. In fact, the earlier you start the better your chances of achieving your financial or retirement goals. Many people make the mistake of starting too late. Don't make the same mistake! You don't need a lot of money to start investing. Start small, start with what you have, meticulously put away a percentage of your income in a savings plan and in no time your investment portfolio will be up and running.

Here are a few tips to get you started

- Sit down with a financial advisor to determine the appropriate investment opportunities for you based on your risk tolerance, age, time horizon and investment objectives.

- What's your risk tolerance? Do you have an appetitive for more risk or less risk? If you are someone who would lose sleep if your stock portfolio suddenly plunges, then the volatile stock market may not be for you.

- If you're less risky, consider investing in safer investments such as fixed income, bonds, blue chip stocks that pays consistent dividends etc. Your returns might be lower but at least you will have peace of mind knowing that your capital will be preserved. If you don't mind taking risk you can invest in growth stocks, penny stocks, precious metals etc. Usually, the greater the risk taken, the higher your potential reward.

- Having a well diversified investment portfolio across different asset classes such as Bonds, Stocks, Commodities and Cash is important in minimizing your risks and maximizing your returns.

- Start sooner. A younger person can afford take more risks as he or she can invest for a longer time period, riding out the down market and profiting from the volatility of the markets. Stock investments are ideal for younger or more risk averse investors as although very risky, stocks in the long term almost always outperforms other asset classes. Older persons or those closer to retirement may not have the luxury of time and may be more focused on playing it safe and preserving their capital and income.

- What's your time horizon? Are you looking to invest for the short term or the long term? Will you be liquidating your investments soon to buy a car, pay down on a home, go on vacation etc. Or, are you locked in for the long haul and saving towards retirement? All these factors will help you determine the type of investment that's suitable for you.

- Rebalance your portfolio. Occasionally you may need to rebalance your portfolio as your investment objectives, risk tolerance, time horizon etc. changes over time. So always check to ensure that you are adjusting your portfolio to suit your changing objectives and circumstances.

PARANDA DAVIS

Ask yourself, what are my short, medium and long-term objectives?

• • • • • • • •

Then start working on a plan towards achieving those goals.

PARANDA DAVIS
Future Planning

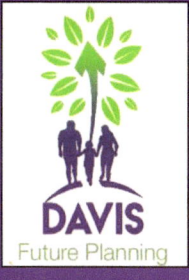

KATIE O'REILLY

Cooking Healthy With Everything Orange

The MILLIONAIRE MAKER *Game*

"Experience Your Fastest Path to Cash!" by Loral Langemeier

PURCHASE LINK:
https://amzn.to/2XItDrU

ANGEL A. WELLINGTON

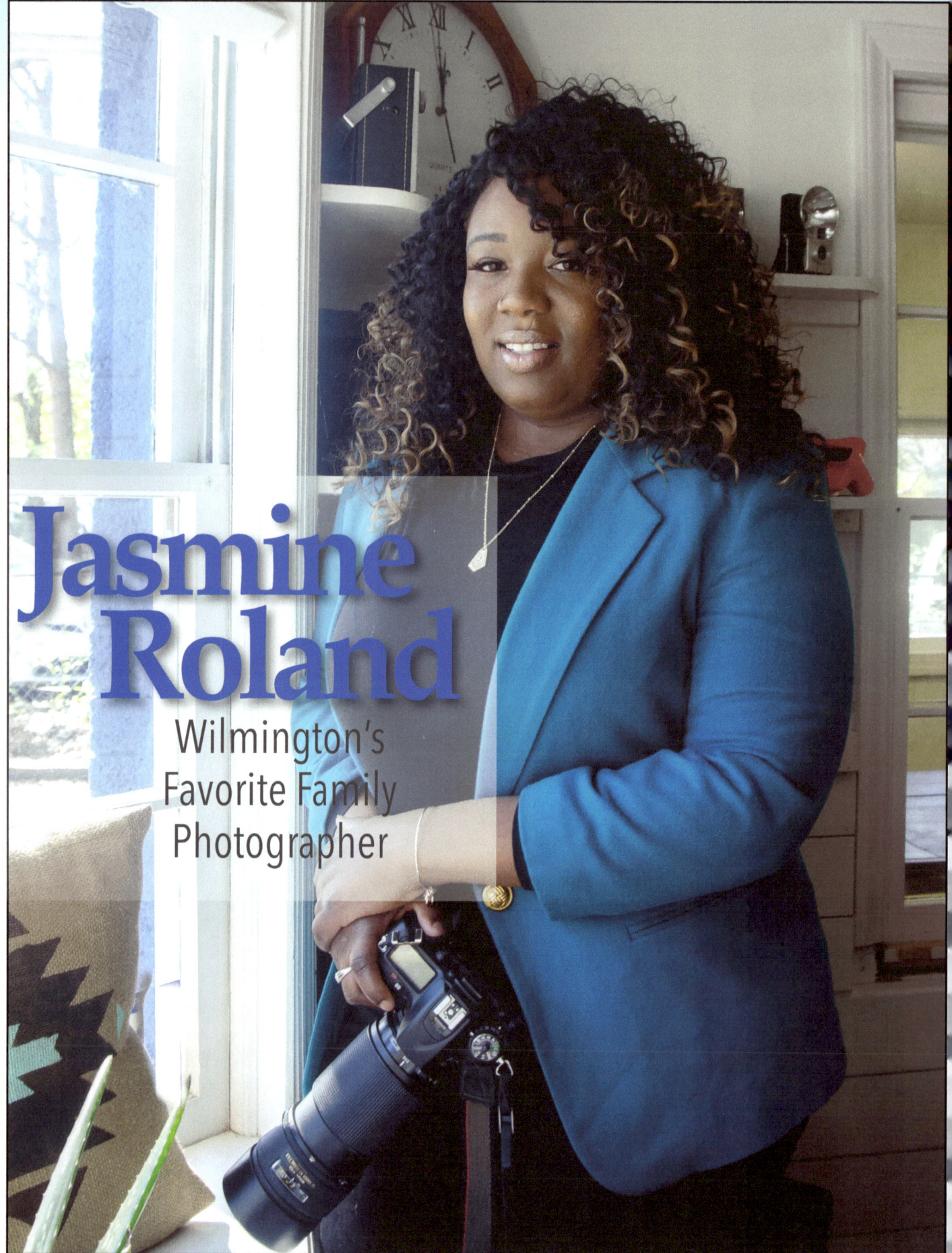

Jasmine Roland

Wilmington's Favorite Family Photographer

"Say Cheese"

ANGEL A. WELLINGTON

The pictures speak for themselves. The soldiers striving to hoist our flag and September 11th firemen doing likewise; Golden Gate and Edmund Pettus bridges, Einstein poking out his tongue and Elvis breaking one knee; Hollywood's sign and Holyfield's dripping ear; Malcolm's and Martin's solemnity; Jackie "O" and Jackie Robinson; "Satchmo's" jaws and Obama's tear, Washington's Lincoln and New York's "Lady" are iconic pictures captured for the sake of keeping us captivated. From patting feet to steaming food, newborns to newlyweds, cruise ships to space ships we want to see it all. Whether drone or GoPro or iPhone, "just take the picture," so we can see the story.

Look back on any photograph and you'll be involuntarily invaded by parts of a surrounding story: the occasion, decorum, scents, fashion, and frozen faces. And the many, many accompanying questions: when was this, why did I wear that, who ended up getting grandma's favorite chair, and where did time go? That's the point after all, making time stop long enough to grab it. Photographic pictures seize the day and photographers take them so that we may repeat each at will. They cause us to remember - even things we would rather forget. But because it is all a part of who we are, the image exists somewhere; attic, treasure chest, scrapbook, cellphone, or cyberspace.

The job of managing our moments seems so sensitive and the person behind a lens so vital. Yet we pay little attention until the interruptive "say cheese." Perhaps we should focus-in on the photographer. We are counting on them after all, since the face behind the camera is responsible for making ours look better.

Of course we would like the universe to believe that we wake up this way. But the reality is proper lighting, careful placement, complimentary background and attention to minuscule detail make the picture. Enter Jasmine Roland. She is the entrepreneurial "eye" seeing what others cannot. The gifted visionary heading her own photography studio (Jazzemup), "Jazz" appreciates depth and dimensional, color and cropping most often missed by untrained "selfie-shooters," "crazy" uncle Bud, or the child who just got a retro Polaroid for his birthday - and is surprised that pictures come out the front.

Voted "Family Favorite Photographer" by Wilmington Parent Magazine, an honor she greatly values

Now the person who does this for a living, Jazz may have begun as any of the aforementioned. A natural knack for taking electronic pictures increased with the arrival of each of her three children. The disposable camera seemed an unlikely means to an end. Determined to document the beginning of their lives, Jazz transformed her home into a studio filled with the necessary backdrop, costumes, props and illumination. The new mom studied everything she could on how professional photographs are taken. She prepped scenes and taught the three

Continued on page 18

ANGEL A. WELLINGTON

"Say Cheese"
Jasmine Roland

Continued from page 17

siblings how to pose in ways that turned-out one exceptional "shoot" after another. It wasn't long before others noticed how different her pictures were to their murky own. The mother-of-invention stoked a passion for photography. The gift of a Nikon D-40 pushed her to explore possibilities.

When a dead-end job failed to yield the potential for financial stability, Jazz had to do something different for her "babies." The business she birthed is all for them. And the rest is their story - and many others - taken one frame at a time. Her thirteen, eleven, and seven year olds share her affinity of photography. Each has identified their own areas of expertise. Sincere, the elder, is quite the photographer in his own right; Tanaziah enjoys assisting with fun shoots (setting up and "cutting up"), Malaki is enthused with his turn before the camera, peeking his head where it otherwise wouldn't belong. He is the unofficial mascot responsible for rendering the subject incapable of not smiling big or laughing loudly. Her "significant other" rounds-out the business partnership celebrating Jazz' success. But they aren't the only ones applauding her efforts. Although her work is requested beyond her immediate vicinity, it is the recent local recognition which Jazz is blessed to have received. Voted "Family Favorite Photographer" by a well-respected area magazine is an honor she greatly values.

Years away from the pangs of working for unappreciative managers or unruly co-workers, Jazz wishes she had known sooner that starting your own business is more work than one could imagine, but greater long-term. It is not easier being "the boss," but for some it works better. Her tip for those beginning from square one, as she did, is it doesn't have to take much capital to just start. Using what you have can get you what you want. "Invest small and build as you prosper." Even getting educated doesn't have to be the expense and insanity it once was. As photography has leaped from throw-aways to storable pictures, learning is no longer confined to classrooms. Find mentors and make yourself an attentive student. "Your success is solely based on you."

She is older, wiser, slower. It is their fifty-fifth anniversary. Walking towards the back door she wishes her feet would keep pace with her desire. She can hardly wait, knowing this gift will "get him" real good. In the seat beside his she flops, laying the book in his bundled lap. No need to ask what it is. The "Our Day" is time tested, but he sees it as he did the day they created the memory. With only the first page flipped he cannot keep his eyes from misting. She reaches for his wrinkled hand, securing it in her own. They go no further. Chins rise to gaze upon the sacred space, their overgrown backyard where the rest of the book took place. There, among the magnolias they promised forever. Here, a photographer gave them back the day. Because that's what good pictures do.

www.jazzemup.info/.

"Say Cheese" Jasmine Roland

Visit me on www.jazzemup.info

ENTREPRENEUR PLATFORM MAGAZINE | 21

"Personal Branding Presence"
RHODA JOHNSON

It is been almost 40 years since I first started helping celebrities, politicians, executives, authors, speakers, and entrepreneurs elevate their careers with my Personal Branding services as a Hollywood Trained Image Consultant and Makeup Artist. See quick video:

https://www.youtube.com/watch?v=Sl-ml7Hv33Q

This amazing journey has evolved into a passion for wellness where I direct my clients into self care as a lifestyle. Over the years I have noticed that the self care lifestyle is vital to radiating true beauty and a magnetic presence.

A magnetic presence is such a gift when networking or speaking because it attracts connection. Non-verbally or energetically, it says you are credible, have high performance habits and a pleasure to be around. It is created by connecting my clients to self care practices, colors, fabrics, styles, and makeup techniques that align with their essence.

When a person shows up consistently with all these elements in place in all their environments, they have a successful Personal Brand. It becomes how they are remembered. Being memorable in a positive way facilitates relationships and new opportunities.

This video demonstrates the power of transformation for a career woman who has been styled with casual business attire, Rhoda De- sign Group gemstone statement jewelry, skincare and makeup. This Spring season makeup is colorful and fresh to celebrate healthy skin:

It is quite extraordinary to see the transformation in my clients as they courageously make the commitment to a new level in the way they show up. They are given Personal Brand tools to become fully aligned with their authentic self. When they stand fully in their power and own their unique gifts unapologetically they exude a quiet confidence that invites others to connect with them.

This is the year of becoming the best version of ourselves. It starts with radical self compassion so we can be more compassionate to others and approach our work from a perspective of life fulfilling purpose. A smile and kindness are the best gifts of ourselves we can give daily that enriches our lives and the lives of others.

Be Well, Be Beautiful,
Rhoda Johnson,
Founder and Creative Visionary of Rhoda Design Group

"DISCOVERING THE AUTHOR WITHIN"
OPHELIA UKE

Soul Empowerer, LLC "DISCOVERING THE AUTHOR WITHIN" Coaching Program was created with you in mind as you've decided to embrace the journey of becoming an author starting with your Objective, to Putting The Pen To Paper until finally we get to the Build Up, which is going to give your readers an insight to "you"! In the End we round off with an…

EXCLUSIVE PERK TO YOU:
A complimentary General Admissions Ticket To My Annual Soul Empowerer 3 Days Retreat/Conference of which I will Showcase you as a New Author!

Writing your first book is about you taking the most important step that is needed in order to "Unleash the Author Within". It's you simply saying "yes" to you and then deciding now is the time to turn your dreams into a reality! I want you to free your mind from every insecurity and discouraging thoughts that may arise, whereby causing you to question your capabilities to accomplish yet another goal which serves to awaken what has laid dormant for so long!

To many, the writing of a book may seem complex, wherein the idea of doing one becomes a scary thought. The process to becoming an author or taking the appropriate steps to writing that first book, which for some may be the first of many, is not as tedious or as complicated as one might think. A book is merely a compilation of one's thoughts or life, simply put into words, which becomes shareable to others. Quite often we become afraid of what we don't know before putting in the work of finding out the details of what it entails.

The purpose of this program is to aide in helping you to develop as an author. The process will help

> *Your goal as the author is to make sure that your reader is able to connect with what they are reading.*

in transforming you into the author you're desiring to become, wherein you're comfortable enough to share your life experiences, your thoughts, emotions, unashamed and unapologetically. Our mission is to get you to understand the direction of the message you are wanting to convey, whereby making the process of writing less daunting so that you can now make your imprint in the world as an Author. You will learn that as an Author/Writer, you must always be in a mindset of preparedness to write down what you may hear or feel at any given moment…this is the beginning of your journey, which will impact the lives of others. What others have felt, you are FINALLY saying.

I extend an Invitation for you to Come Work With Me So The Journey Of You Being An Author Can Begin! Every word written within the chapters

Continued on page 28

NIKKI MURRILL

Dotcom Secrets Book Review

I first learned about the author of Dotcom Secrets, Russell Brunson, on YouTube. Back in 2011 or so, Russell Brunson had a system for online entrepreneurs to follow in order to earn commissions as an affiliate marketer. He earned my respect then and has continued to hold my attention with the release of Dotcom Secrets as well as other well-known and fine products. Let's delve in!

My sole purpose for reading this book was to learn how to make money online. I went from searching the web, early mornings while breastfeeding, for topics such as weight loss after pregnancy to topics of how to make supplemental income online. Affiliate marketing is the model that has stuck with me ever since.

Affiliate Marketing and Dotcom Secrets

Russell Brunson shares so profoundly in his book the power of connecting your target audience with a product they are willing to spend money for. In return, you earn a commission! That is affiliate marketing. This author is well qualified to teach success in this realm as he studied junk mail as a kid. That is rare and seems very odd! Since then, he has ascertained understanding of the human psyche, the effectiveness of copywriting, and how to leverage a traffic funnel.

A traffic funnel or funnel is the process by which a marketer leads their potential customer or client from inception to ultimately the sale. Unfortunately, funnels can be complicated beasts and are not all designed to be fly-by-night successes.

Russell teaches the establishment of a relationship with your market and in exchange for value, you can engage and hopefully gain trust enough to profit. This can take a short period of time or several weeks and beyond. An example of a marketing funnel is McDonald's has a viral tee-shirt than can only be found on their website. You hear about the shirt on an advertisement on YouTube. To purchase the shirt, you would click through to the sales page on the McDonald's website.

If done right, Brunson teaches, a proper funnel can earn you more than what you invested in. An impressive formula he uses in the book is earn $2 for every $1 you spend.

Dotcom Secrets on Website Traffic

Every public site on the World Wide Web has been placed there so that others can interact with it. Daily visitors to websites is known as traffic. Russell Brunson elaborates in Dotcom Secrets how those with an entrepreneurial mindset can capitalize on web traffic especially with the competition being so astronomical.

I learned about website traffic eight years ago after publishing my first website. I searched in Google in hopes to find it among search results and it was nowhere to be found! Over the years I have endeavored to master this method.

Though my first attempt failed, we know that a website can receive organic traffic by visitors who find your site in the search engine results on platforms such as Bing, Google, or YouTube. Social media traffic also facilitates tons of website traffic. Writing a blog post on my personal blog and then sharing it on Twitter can produce new followers and give my existing followers more content to click through to and enjoy. Another type of website traffic is paid traffic. This can be through Google, Bing, YouTube, Tonic, Snapchat, Propeller Ads or any other medium that can place your advertisement before the eyes of many for a fee.

Russell illuminates the necessity of any entrepreneur who publishes on a web property to own their traffic. His book delineates how to transform website visitors, whether paid or organically generated, into vibrant subscribers to your website content: blog posts, pictures, ads, newsletters, videos, and more. This information is pivotal for any business owner because this is how you generate revenue.

The digital marketing space hails Russell Brunson as a genius as he has broken down the major problems and provided solutions that many struggle with as beginners or even the experienced. His teachings on how to scope out your competition and use their success as leverage in building your own empire has been priceless. His product Clickfunnels brings to life the book Dotcom Secrets with the application of funnel building. This technology enables the user to capture leads and take them on a journey to the sale and hopefully establishes an ongoing business relationship. Now that is traffic you own!

Dotcom Secrets: My Take Away

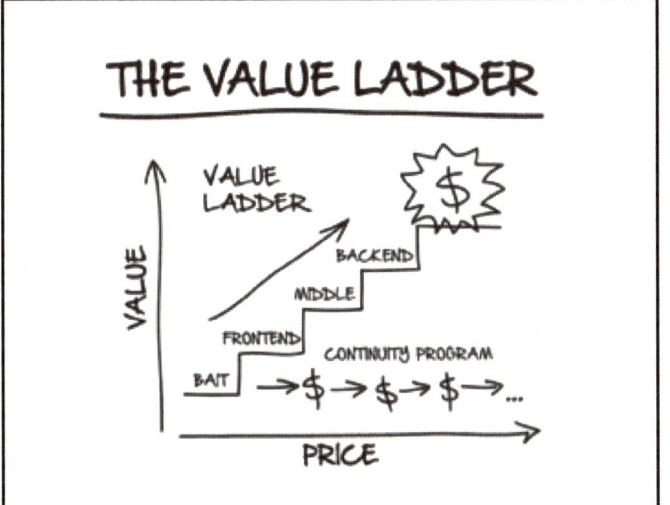

I cherished most his term in Dotcom Secrets called the "Attractive Character". I identify with this because I am on the marketing team for my husband, a professional saxophonist. In reading this book, I learned that my husband's presence on platforms like YouTube, Instagram, facebook, to name a few, can help brand him and win the hearts of others who aspire to be like him or simply enjoy his music and instruction. He is that attractive character. I immediately went to my husband after reading this book and explained how he could someday create his own products using Russell's funnel pictured above. He is now coming in to the full grasp of how lucrative being an attractive character is as it relates to business and entrepreneurship. We have not launched a product yet, but offerings like Dotcom Secrets make the process a whole lot more appealing and scalable!

To purchase Dotcom Secrets visit Russell Brunson's website. There you can order the 255 page book absolutely free and just pay a nominal amount of $7.95 for shipping and handling. It will be worth it! Russell Brunson has sold almost 100,000 copies and Dotcom Secrets is an USA Today & Amazon Best Seller!

Nikki Murrill is a proud mother of four fabulous children, wife of a preacher/musician, a school teacher, and a freelance writer. To read more of her work, visit her blog at http://nikkimurrill.com.

ENTREPRENEUR PLATFORM Magazine
Available as digital and print

Continued from page 7

Elinor Stutz

Do You Take Risks to Reach New Heights?

Sales Tips for Chances to Reach New Heights

1. When offers come your way, examine possibilities from multiple angles
2. Prioritize what needs to get done
3. Create and prioritize your wish list
4. Stick to a strict timeline for accomplishing everything you prioritize
5. Set goals with deadlines to efficiently complete each task and project
6. As you approach achieving one goal, target a more difficult one
7. Seek out people with similar interests and a collaborative style
8. Review all processes regularly and ensure all work in unison
9. Every six months attempt one new goal somewhat over your capability
10. **Celebrate Success!**

ELINOR STUTZ

ENTREPRENEUR PLATFORM MAGAZINE AVAILABLE IN EITHER DIGITAL OR PRINT

Issuu

Amazon Shopping

Continued from page 5

Thriving In Uncertainty

5 Strategies to Succeed No Matter What this Economy Does

your ability to build relationships. But not relationships like you have known in the past – this is relationships on steroids. You have to create a prospect experience that is so amazing they do not think they can find it anywhere else, and then pro-actively add value to your existing customers so they believe they cannot live without you.

5. Get Your Head Out Of The Sand – There is more going on in this economy than what is happening in your business. In the age of uncertainty there are far more changes happening outside of your business that could impact your success then are happening in it.

To be thrive you need to routinely get your head out of the sand and take a look around. Every three or four months, get together with your team or your peers and ask: What is happening in the world around you? What is changing with consumers? How is your industry responding and growing? What is happening politically? What societal trends could positively or negatively impact your business? Understanding, pro-actively, what is happening in the bigger picture puts you in the power seat to minimize challenges and seize on opportunity.

You know change is coming – if you see it is creating opportunity, keep your head in the sand and it becomes your biggest threat.

Today's marketplace is nothing if not challenging, but I still believe it is one of the best times to be in business, and one of the best to be successful. By using these strategies - Embrace Reality, Focus On Values, Build Your Image, Invest In Relationships and Get Your Head Out of The Sand, you will position your team to thrive in uncertainty and succeed no matter what this economy does.

Voted One of The Top 15 Business Growth Experts To Watch, and A Top 40 Motivational Speaker, Meridith Elliott Powell share the strategies you need to understand today's marketplace and put yourself in a position to Thrive In Uncertainty. To learn more, get free trips, to talk with Meridith mere@valuespeaker.com

Website: https://www.meridithelliottpowell.com/
FaceBook: https://www.facebook.com/MeridithElliotPowell/
LinkedIn: https://www.linkedin.com/in/meridithelliottpowell
Twitter: https://twitter.com/meridithpowell
YouTube: https://www.youtube.com/user/meridithepowell

Meridith Elliott Powell

Business Keynote Speaker & Business Growth Expert

Creating Ownership At Every Level; Profits At Every Turn

Continued from page 23

OPHELIA UKE
"DISCOVERING THE AUTHOR WITHIN"

of your book will be your own, as it is you writing it, not me. Know this, your experiences are the beginning to someone else's healing. Today, let's begin the journey to you Becoming An Author!

One of our goals is to make certain you are comfortable with your message and that you are in control of your thoughts and what it is that you are feeling. Your goal as the author is to make sure that your reader is able to connect with what they are reading. Even though it may be your life, and your story it's really not about you… it becomes about the person who has decided to read the book you have written because it is now their self-help guide to becoming a better them, to understanding their purpose, or to make them feel something they have never before felt.

Be kind, for everyone you meet is fighting a hard battle.
-- Tahir Hussain

Consultants

Paranda Davis
Davis Future Planning, LLC
Credit Repair - Personal
Build Business Credit
Business Loans
www.davisfutureplanning.com
P: 800-239-1493
FREE CONSULTATION

Karen Albert
Behind Your Curtain
Social Media Consultant - Business & Personal
Digital Strategy Expert
https://behindyourcurtain.com
FREE CONSULTATION

Ophelia Nixon Uke
Soul Empowerer, LLC
"Discovering The Author Within"
Book Writing & Publishing
www.soulempowerer.com
P: 845-244-0510
FREE CONSULTATION

Rhoda Johnson
The Rhoda Design Group
Professional Business Image Consultant
https://rhodadesigngroup.com
P: 303-755-2345
FREE CONSULTATION

Want to be featured on our cover?
Be a Contributing Writer, advertise your business, products, services, tutorials or books to a global audience?

Contact us at: entrepreneurplatformmagazine@gmail.com

BOOKS OF THE MONTH

Entrepreneurial Books of the Month

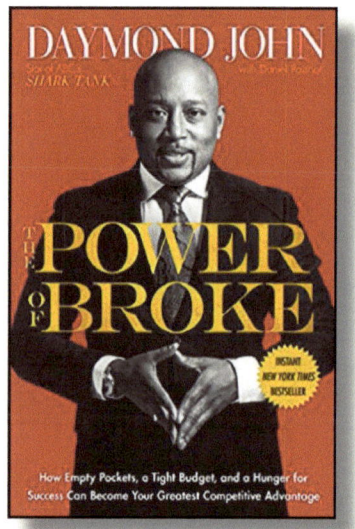

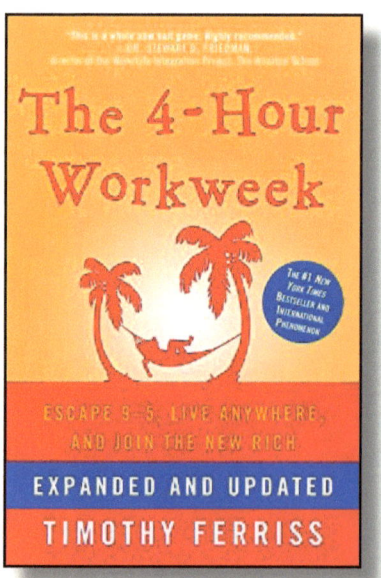

32 | ENTREPRENEUR PLATFORM MAGAZINE

Ripple and XRP

ENTREPRENEUR PLATFORM MAGAZINE | 33

www.ingramcontent.com/pod-product-compliance
Lightning Source LLC
Chambersburg PA
CBHW041300180526
45172CB00003B/912